CENTAURUS

CRUX

LUPUS

MUSCA

NORMA

CIRCINUS

TRIANGULUM AUSTRALE

APUS

ARA

OCTANS

To Mum and Dad,
for helping a little girl dream big.
—T.H.

For my dad, Maris, who has always
encouraged me to look with curiosity:
paldies, danke, thank you.
—S.M.

First published in 2024 by
Museums Victoria Publishing

11 Nicholson Street
Carlton, Victoria 3053, Australia
publications@museum.vic.gov.au

www.museumsvictoria.com.au

Text by Tanya Hill © Museums Victoria
Ilustrations by Sylvia Morris © Sylvia Morris

A catalogue record for this book is available from the National Library of Australia.

ISBN 9781921833694

Design by Julia Donkersley
Production by Sasha Beekman
Printed in China by RR Donnelley Asia Printing Solutions, Ltd.

1 3 5 7 9 10 8 6 4 2

Museums Victoria acknowledges the Wurundjeri Woi Wurrung and Boon Wurrung peoples of the eastern Kulin Nations where we work, and First Peoples language groups and communities across Victoria and Australia. Our organisation, in partnership with the First Peoples of Victoria, is working to place First Peoples living cultures and histories at the core of our practice.

This book has been created by Museums Victoria, Australia's largest public museum organisation. Our venues include Melbourne Museum, Scienceworks, Immigration Museum and Royal Exhibition Building. Proceeds from the sale of this book support Museums Victoria's collections and ongoing research.

TANYA HILL

SYLVIA MORRIS

Every Friday, Lily's family went walking after dinner.

Sometimes they'd walk through the park, where the trees reached their branches high above Lily.

Sometimes they'd walk around their neighbourhood, shouting, 'Hello!' to all the people out and about enjoying the evening.

KEEP LEFT
HELLOooooooooooo!

Sometimes Lily's family would walk between the tall buildings of the city.

At other times, their walks took them into wide, open fields.
When Lily looked up, there was only the bright blue sky as far as she could see.

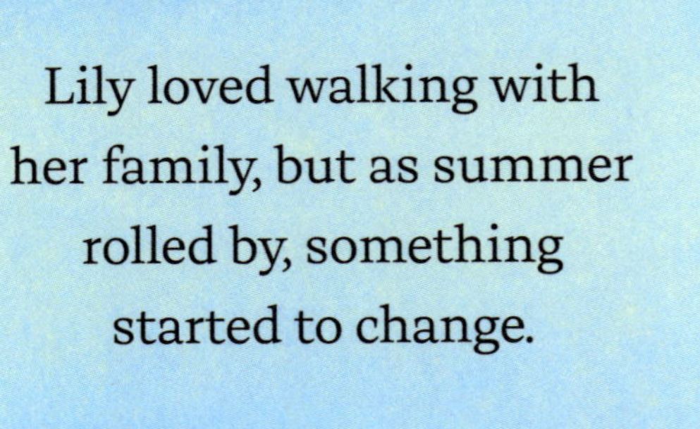

Lily loved walking with her family, but as summer rolled by, something started to change.

Each week, as they arrived back home, Lily noticed the Sun had sunk a little bit closer to the horizon.

The sky was changing too.
No longer bright blue,
the colour was fading away.
It was becoming darker.

And that was
a problem, because ...

… Lily was scared of the dark.

She didn't like how it did strange things to the world around her.
Shadows loomed and stretched, tiny creaks and noises became much too loud.

Lily would lie awake at night, waiting for morning to come and for the Sun to chase the darkness away.

Summer soon became autumn, and one Friday, while the rest of the family talked and laughed over dinner, Lily stayed very quiet.

As the family left home, Lily kept her head down. She knew sunset was coming and the Sun was about to disappear below the horizon. Soon it would be getting dark.

Lily stared at her toes, frightened of what she might see if she looked up.

Then suddenly …

Lily's brother had stopped still and was pointing straight up at something high overhead.

‘Mum,’ he shouted,
‘Look at that bright star!’

‘That might look like a star,’ said Lily’s mum, ‘but it’s actually the largest planet in the solar system—the planet Jupiter’.

Lily sneaked a quick glance up at the sky.
Was it really possible to see a planet
like Jupiter with her own eyes?

A few blocks later, Lily's sister exclaimed, 'Mum! I can see a star that's moving across the sky!' Lily's mum looked up.

'Guess what? That's not a star either—it's the International Space Station. That's where astronauts from around the world come together to live and work and teach us about being in space.'

‘I wonder what they might be having for dinner?’ said Lily’s mum, laughing.

Picturing astronauts eating together in space made Lily smile too—just a little bit.

As Lily's family headed home,
the last light of day was fading fast.
It was getting darker, and Lily was
growing more afraid than ever.

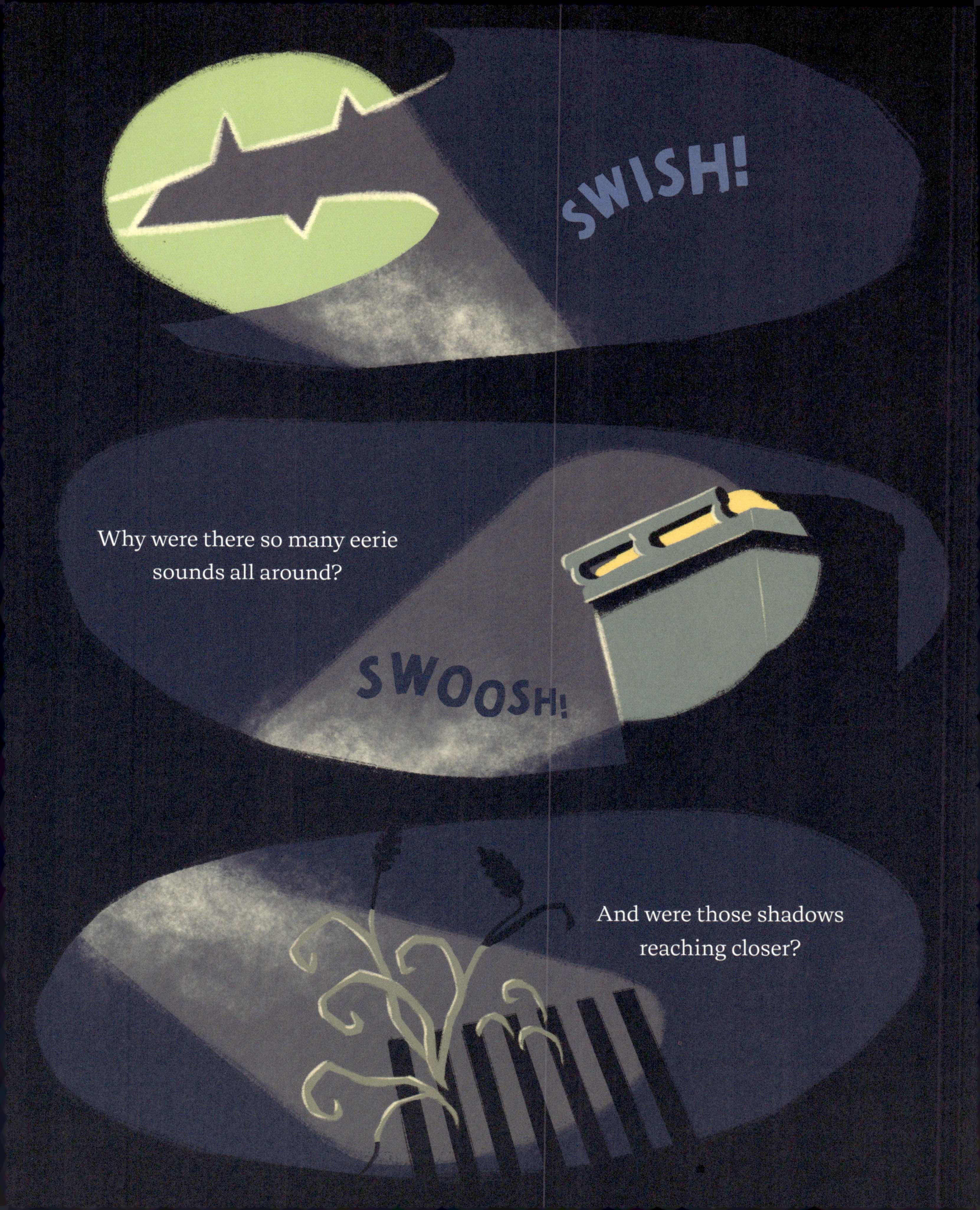

SWISH!

Why were there so many eerie sounds all around?

SWOOSH!

And were those shadows reaching closer?

Lily's steps grew smaller,
and her legs began to shake.

Suddenly she felt a warm hand upon her shoulder.
'Lily,' her mum said quietly. 'Look.'

Lily looked up ...

… and there, right in front of her,
was the magnificent full Moon.

'Look at all the stars, Lily.
Isn't the night beautiful?'

Lily's mum pointed to three little stars lined up in a row. 'They're part of Orion, the mighty hunter,' she said. 'Follow those stars and you'll find the brightest star in the night sky—Sirius, the dog star.'

Lily stared at the sky above. As she watched the night grow darker and darker, the stars began shining brighter and brighter. The longer she looked, the more stars she could see.

SIRIUS

PROCYON

RIGEL

ORION

BETELGEUSE

BELLATRIX

ALDEBARAN

For the first time in her life,
Lily saw that the night WAS beautiful.

Lily had so many questions.
There was so much she wanted to learn!

Why did the stars shine so brightly?
And how come, as the seasons changed,
she could see different stars in the sky?

What stories could the constellations tell her?
And where did all the stories come from?

Lily isn't scared of the dark anymore. She still enjoys walking after dinner with her family each week, but now her favourite thing is going camping and spending the whole night outdoors.

In the wide, open fields, with darkness all around her,
Lily knows that the sparkling stars are always there too.
All she needs to do is look up.

TANYA'S STORY

Dr Tanya Hill is the senior curator of astronomy at the Melbourne Planetarium at Scienceworks. She's worked at the planetarium since it first opened in 1999, creating award-winning planetarium shows that are shown all around the world.

Tanya loves astronomy and being able to explore the universe, but it wasn't always like that. When she was a little girl, Tanya was scared of the dark. It was her dad who put his hand on her shoulder and encouraged her to look up at the stars—at the Southern Cross especially—and she's been looking up ever since.

Tanya had her first chance to look through a telescope in high school, and she was amazed at how many more stars she could see. But it wasn't until she started studying physics at university that Tanya was able to meet and work with some remarkable astronomers—people who explored the universe as their profession. One astronomer in particular, Dr Charlene Heisler, was especially encouraging and showed Tanya that she could become an astronomer too. Together, Tanya and Charlene studied faraway galaxies, searching for supermassive black holes, and this research earned Tanya her PhD.

Tanya enjoys sharing all that is known about the universe with planetarium audiences, but her favourite people to share the universe with are her husband Alex and her three sons—Dylan, Nathan and Damien. Heading home one winter's night, Tanya pointed out the International Space Station to her boys. They asked the most important question of all: 'Mum, do astronauts get to eat spaghetti bolognaise for dinner, just like us?'

LEPUS

CANIS MAJOR

ERIDANUS

ORION

MONOCEROS

CANIS MINOR

TAURUS

GEMINI

AURIGA